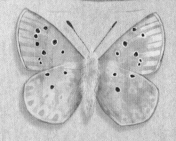

# A Children's Guide to
# Arctic Butterflies

by Mia Pelletier

illustrated by Danny Christopher

INHABIT
MEDIA

For the little ones of the North. May butterflies adorn the paths you travel.

Published by Inhabit Media Inc.
www.inhabitmedia.com

Inhabit Media Inc. (Iqaluit) P.O. Box 11125, Iqaluit, Nunavut, X0A 1H0
(Toronto) 191 Eglinton Avenue East, Suite 310, Toronto, Ontario, M4P 1K1

This project was made possible in part by the Government of Canada.

We acknowledge the support of the Canada Council for the Arts for our publishing program.

Printed in Canada

Library and Archives Canada Cataloguing in Publication

Title: A children's guide to Arctic butterflies / by Mia Pelletier ; illustrated by Danny
    Christopher.
Names: Pelletier, Mia, author. | Christopher, Danny, 1975- illustrator.
Identifiers: Canadiana 20190116366 | ISBN 9781772271775 (hardcover)
Subjects: LCSH: Butterflies—Arctic regions—Identification—Juvenile literature. | LCSH: Butterflies—
    Arctic regions—Juvenile literature. | LCGFT: Field guides.
Classification: LCC QL560 .P45 2019 | DDC j595.780911/3—dc23

# Table of Contents

# Introduction

When we think of Arctic animals, we tend to imagine polar bears with their thick, woolly coats, or walruses and seals with their warm layers of blubber, not delicate summer creatures like butterflies. Yet butterflies are found in almost every corner of the world, from the hot, steamy tropics to the vast, frozen tundra at the top of the world.

Of the 20,000 species of butterflies in the world, only several dozen can be found on the tundra of the North American Arctic. Just seven are found as far north as the High Arctic islands in Nunavut. From the cool, windy summers to the long, icy winters, these hardy butterflies must have clever ways of surviving from one Arctic season to the next!

When we go searching for small and secretive wild creatures, the first step is learning how to look. Like an intricate painting, the endless, seemingly empty Arctic landscape invites us closer to notice the tiny details that define the open space: the pattern of lichen on a tundra rock, the lace of frost on a willow leaf, a single feather glittering with dew. Often hidden from sight with their camouflaged wings, Arctic butterflies give us a reason to slow our steps and *look closer*. Up close, we find that the tundra is not empty at all, but teeming with unexpected life. A copper butterfly gleams as it spreads its shining wings. A sulphur butterfly folds its pastel-coloured wings, almost vanishing into stone. When we step back, the subtle colours, textures, and patterns of Arctic life fill the landscape, and we find that our view is forever changed.

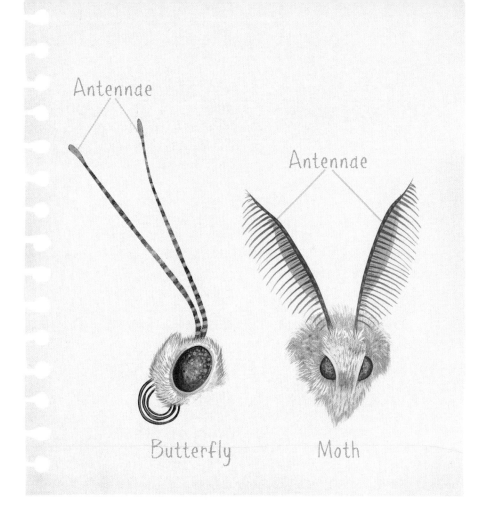

Antennae

Antennae

Butterfly

Moth

# A Butterfly or a Moth?

Many people think of butterflies as bright-coloured, sun-loving insects and moths as dull-coloured insects that fly only at night. However, there are hundreds of colourful moth species, some of which fly during the day, and thousands of dull-coloured butterflies. So how can we tell them apart? One way is to look at their antennae. Butterflies typically have straight, thin antennae with "knobby" tips. Moths usually have feathery or fine-tipped antennae. Also, butterflies do not spin silky cocoons like moths do. They change from caterpillars to butterflies inside of a hard-shelled chrysalis.

# Parts of a Butterfly

EYES: A butterfly can see and sense movement in almost every direction without even moving its head! Butterflies see in colour. They can also see ultraviolet light, a kind of light that is invisible to humans.

ANTENNAE: A butterfly's antennae are highly sensitive and can be moved about in all directions like bendy straws. Butterflies "smell" with their antennae and use them to navigate their environment, to find food, and to help identify mates.

PROBOSCIS: The proboscis is a sipping tube that acts like a tongue. It can be coiled up like a spring when it is not in use and uncoiled to reach deep inside flowers to drink their hidden nectar.

THORAX: The thorax protects the butterfly like armour. It also anchors the legs and wings to the body. Inside, powerful muscles move the butterfly's wings up and down—up to 20 beats per second for some butterflies!

LEGS: Butterflies have three pairs of jointed legs with special "taste buds" on their feet. These help them find the right kinds of plants to lay their eggs on.

WINGS: Butterflies have two pairs of overlapping wings: forewings and hindwings. The wings are made of a strong, see-through membrane that is covered in a dusty layer of small, flat scales. The scales overlap and reflect light to produce the many different colours of a butterfly's wings. The colours and patterns on the upper side of the wings are usually quite different from those on the underside. A network of tiny veins supports the wings.

ABDOMEN: The tough, flexible abdomen holds the heart and the organs for digestion and mating. Butterflies breathe through tiny holes in the abdomen.

Forewings

Antennae

Thorax

Abdomen

Hindwings

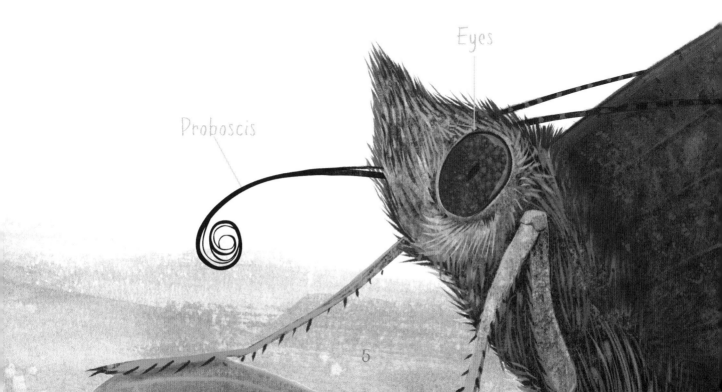

Eyes

Proboscis

5

# THE BUTTERFLY LIFE CYCLE

There are four stages in a butterfly's life cycle: egg, caterpillar, chrysalis, and adult butterfly. The amazing process that takes an egg through to becoming a butterfly is called "metamorphosis."

EGG: Caterpillars can typically only eat one or a few kinds of plants. For this reason, female butterflies take their time selecting just the right kind of food plant to lay their eggs on. Eggs are often laid on the underside of leaves, where they are sheltered from the weather.

CATERPILLAR: Once hatched from its egg, a caterpillar's most important jobs are to survive, eat, and GROW! A caterpillar can increase in weight up to 15,000 times between when it hatches and when it enters its chrysalis! As it grows, a caterpillar's skin stretches until it is shed and replaced by a looser skin that grows underneath. When a caterpillar has finished growing, its last skin splits to reveal a hard-shelled chrysalis.

CHRYSALIS: The chrysalis is a tough case that protects the caterpillar as it transforms into a butterfly. The chrysalis is often shaped or coloured to blend in with natural things, like leaves or bark. When the butterfly's metamorphosis is complete, the chrysalis splits, and a rumpled, wet-winged butterfly crawls out.

BUTTERFLY: Once its wings dry, a butterfly can take flight. In the Arctic, butterflies are usually seen flying in late June, July, and early August. Vulnerable to predators and changing weather, most butterflies live short lives of only a couple of weeks. During this brief time, butterflies must find a mate, lay their eggs, and begin the cycle anew.

Eggs

Caterpillar

Chrysalis

Butterfly

## Staying Warm in the Arctic

Unlike birds or mammals, butterflies are cold-blooded. This means that they need to warm their bodies with the heat of the sun or air in order to fly. Holding their wings at angles to the sun, butterflies use their wings like solar panels to capture the sun's heat. This is called "basking." Some types of butterflies have shiny wings that they use like mirrors to reflect sunlight onto their thorax.

Butterflies that live in the Arctic are typically darker and "hairier" than those found farther south. Dark colours soak up more of the sun's warmth. The "hair" traps a warm layer of air close to the body. Butterflies climb up onto sunny rocks and plants to find the best spots to bask. They also press their bodies against the sun-warmed ground. On blustery days, butterflies fly low to the ground where the air is calmer and seek sheltered places to escape the wind.

# What Do Arctic Butterflies Do in the Winter?

In places where summers are long and mild, a caterpillar can develop into a butterfly in a single summer. But Arctic summers are short and cool, and caterpillars grow more slowly. Many species need more than one, and sometimes even two, summers to become butterflies. You might wonder how a soft, squishy caterpillar can survive the icy Arctic winter—wouldn't they freeze solid? The truth is, some do!

Butterflies survive the Arctic winter in a kind of hibernating state called "diapause." Different kinds of butterflies hibernate in different life stages, but many Arctic species hibernate as caterpillars. In this state, everything in a caterpillar's body slows almost to a stop, as if time stands still while winter passes. When spring arrives, the caterpillar thaws and wakes. Picking up where it left off, it continues to eat and grow! Arctic butterflies can also produce a kind of "antifreeze." This prevents ice from forming in the fragile tissues in their bodies.

10

# Arctic Butterflies

# PALAENO SULPHUR
## COLIAS PALAENO

 Wingspan: 32 to 45 mm

Upper Side

Underside

The Palaeno Sulphur is a handsome butterfly. It has bright yellow wings with wide, black wing borders. The female's wings are lighter coloured, with thin black borders. On the underside, the wings are greenish yellow with a pink fringe. The hindwings have a thick dusting of dark scales and a small, white spot in the centre. Palaeno Sulphurs that live on Baffin Island are darker than those found farther south.

WHERE TO LOOK: Palaeno Sulphurs are found on the open tundra from Alaska to the coast of Labrador. They live as far north as Victoria and Baffin Islands. This butterfly prefers sheltered stream valleys and is often seen near blueberry plants.

HOW THEY FLY: Palaeno Sulphurs fly close to the ground with a fast, darting flight.

CATERPILLAR: The caterpillars are green with a yellow stripe running down each side. They like to eat Arctic blueberry and dwarf blueberry leaves.

DURING THE WINTER: Palaeno Sulphur caterpillars "sleep" through the winter in diapause and form a chrysalis the following summer. Using antifreeze compounds to protect themselves from frost, they are able to resist freezing in temperatures as low as -25°C!

FLUTTERING FACT: Together with their cousins, the moths, butterflies make up a group of insects called *Lepidoptera*. This is a Latin word that means "scaly wings." This name refers to the thousands of tiny scales that cover a butterfly's wings and give them their rainbow of beautiful colours.

# LABRADOR SULPHUR
*Colias nastes*

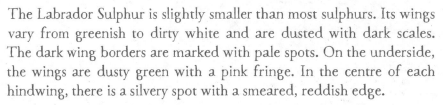

Wingspan: 28 to 42 mm

Upper Side

Underside

The Labrador Sulphur is slightly smaller than most sulphurs. Its wings vary from greenish to dirty white and are dusted with dark scales. The dark wing borders are marked with pale spots. On the underside, the wings are dusty green with a pink fringe. In the centre of each hindwing, there is a silvery spot with a smeared, reddish edge.

WHERE TO LOOK: Labrador Sulphurs are found on the tundra from Alaska to Labrador and as far north as any butterfly in the world: on Ellesmere Island in Nunavut! Labrador Sulphurs prefer rocky, windy ridges and gravelly hilltops. Their greenish wings make these butterflies quite difficult to spot on the tundra. When they bask, their wings closed and tilted sideways to face the sun, they almost seem to disappear!

HOW THEY FLY: The Labrador Sulphur flies low over the ground with a fast, moth-like flight.

CATERPILLAR: Labrador Sulphur caterpillars are green. They have lighter green stripes on the side that are bordered in red. They like to eat plants in the pea family, like alpine milk-vetch.

DURING THE WINTER: Mature caterpillars hibernate for one winter. They change into butterflies the following summer.

FLUTTERING FACT: While caterpillars only eat certain plants, most butterflies drink nectar from a variety of flowers. Some kinds of butterflies even feed on carrion, dung, sweat, sap, rotting fruit, or minerals found in wet soil.

# Hecla Sulphur
*Colias hecla*

 Wingspan: 33 to 45 mm

Upper Side

Underside

The Hecla Sulphur has striking, dark orange wings with black borders. It has dark scales near the body and a brighter orange spot in the centre of each hindwing. Females have more dark scales than the males. They also have orange spots in their wing borders. On the underside, the wings are greenish. There is a silver spot ringed with pink on each of the hindwings. A red streak that looks like a comet's tail runs from this spot toward the wing's outer edge.

**Where to Look:** A common butterfly in the far North, the Hecla Sulphur can be found on wet Arctic tundra from Alaska to the coast of Labrador and as far north as Ellesmere Island. Look closely, and you might spot them basking with their wings closed and tilted sideways to catch the sun's rays. Like other Arctic sulphurs, their pastel-coloured wings are dulled by darker scaling underneath. This helps them absorb the sun's heat.

**How They Fly:** Hecla Sulphurs fly quickly over the tundra, staying close to the ground where the air is calmer.

**Caterpillar:** These caterpillars are slim, green, and fuzzy. They have light-coloured stripes running down their bodies. They like to eat plants in the pea family, especially alpine milk-vetch.

**During the Winter:** Butterflies of the far North, like the Hecla Sulphur, are less studied than many southern species. However, like many northern butterflies, the Hecla Sulphur is thought to take two years to develop into an adult butterfly. It hibernates as a caterpillar through the first winter and forms a chrysalis the following summer.

**Fluttering Fact:** No one is quite sure where the word "butterfly" came from. Some say that the buttery yellow colour of European sulphur butterflies was the inspiration for the word "butter-fly." Other stories claim that the word used to be "flutter-by." Some say that witches were thought to take on the shape of butterflies and steal milk and butter during the night!

# American Copper

*Lycaena phlaeas*

Wingspan: 21 to 30 mm

Upper Side

The American Copper is a small, brightly coloured butterfly. It has shiny, yellow-orange forewings with black spots and a grey border. Its dusky, grey-brown hindwings are bordered in orange. On the underside, the hindwings are light grey with black spots and a thin, wavy orange line near the outer edge.

Underside

**Where to Look:** American Coppers are found on the tundra from Alaska to Nunavut as far north as the northern tip of Ellesmere Island. They are often seen near their favourite nectar or caterpillar food plants. Look for them as they bask or rest on flowers with their wings open and shining in the sun.

**How They Fly:** American Coppers are fast fliers. They fly in short bursts from one flower or perch to another.

**Caterpillar:** American Copper caterpillars are covered in downy hairs. They can vary in colour from reddish to yellow-green with white to red stripes. They like to eat mountain sorrel.

**During the Winter:** The American Copper hibernates through the winter as a chrysalis. The adult butterfly emerges the following summer.

**Fluttering Fact:** The American Copper is one of the most aggressive butterflies in its family. Males can be very territorial, often chasing other butterflies away. They've even been known to chase passing shadows or falling leaves!

# Arctic Blue
## *Agriades glandon*

 Wingspan: 17 to 23 mm

Upper Side

Underside

Arctic Blues are small butterflies that vary in colour. The more northern blues are both smaller and darker than those found farther south and may sometimes be mistaken for moths. Males have dark grey-blue wings with grey borders. Females have wings that are dark grey or grey-brown. Both males and females have dark bars near the outer edge of their wings, bordered by light grey. A row of ringed dark spots marks the outer edges of the hindwings. On the underside, the wings are grey with many white-ringed spots that look like eyes.

**Where to Look:** Arctic Blues are found from Alaska to the coast of Labrador and north as far as Ellesmere Island. They prefer open, dry tundra and mountain habitats. Arctic Blues are often seen fluttering around their food plants and sitting on flowers. Their dusky-coloured wings can make them quite difficult to spot when they rest on the ground.

**How They Fly:** Although many blues are weak fliers, Arctic Blues have a fast, zigzag flight. They fly close to the ground, but when startled, they will lift up into the air and let themselves be carried away on the wind.

**Caterpillar:** Arctic Blue caterpillars are light green with reddish markings and are covered with long, downy hair. Caterpillars eat the buds and flowers of their food plants, which may include the pincushion plant, the crowberry plant, and purple saxifrage.

**During the Winter:** Arctic Blues hibernate as a chrysalis during their first winter and change into butterflies the following summer.

**Fluttering Fact:** The many eye-like spots on the underside of the Arctic Blue's wings give this butterfly part of its scientific name, *Agriades glandon*. The Latin name *Agriades* means "like Argus," a mythical giant who had 100 eyes!

# CRANBERRY BLUE
*VACCINIINA OPTILETE*

 Wingspan: 18 to 24 mm

Upper Side

Underside

The Cranberry Blue is a small butterfly with striking, dark purple-blue wings. The female's wings are browner, with only a blush of purple at the base. Unlike the males, they also have wide, dark wing borders. On the underside, the Cranberry Blue's wings are pale grey with two rows of large, dark spots on both wings. The spots in the inner row are ringed with white scales. The largest spot on each of the hindwings is marked with orange.

WHERE TO LOOK: Although more common in the western Arctic, the Cranberry Blue can be found from Alaska to mainland Nunavut. These butterflies prefer wet tundra and boggy areas where their food plants grow. True to their name, they are often seen near cranberry plants, and can also be found near blueberry plants. Some kinds of butterflies, including the blues and sulphurs, like to sip on salts and other minerals found in the mud. This means that the muddy edges of ponds and puddles can be good places to spot blue butterflies!

HOW THEY FLY: Cranberry Blues are weak fliers and tend to fly quite close to the ground.

CATERPILLAR: The Cranberry Blue caterpillar has not yet been described in North America. However, in Scandinavia, it has been described as being green and furry with pale yellow lines running down each side. These caterpillars like to eat blueberry and cranberry plants.

DURING THE WINTER: Partly grown caterpillars hibernate during the winter and continue their life cycle the following spring.

FLUTTERING FACT: There is still a lot of mystery in the world of caterpillars! Quite a few of the caterpillars in North America have never even been seen in the wild. As well, caterpillars of the same species can be different colours, and in most species, the younger caterpillars look much different than the older caterpillars.

# Frigga Fritillary
*Boloria frigga*

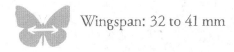 Wingspan: 32 to 41 mm

Upper Side

Underside

The Frigga Fritillary is a medium-sized butterfly. Its golden orange-brown wings are patterned with dark marks. The wings are darker at the base and have rows of dark spots near the outer edges. On the underside, the hindwings have a dark base followed by a golden band. There is a broad, purplish band along the outer edge and a large white patch on the upper edge. Frigga Fritillaries that live on the Arctic tundra are both larger and more yellow than those found farther south.

WHERE TO LOOK: Frigga Fritillaries are found from Alaska east through most of Arctic Canada. They can be found as far north as northern Baffin Island. They prefer wet, shrubby places on the tundra, such as willow bogs. Frigga Fritillaries have been spotted laying their eggs on mountain avens plants. They bask with their wings spread open, so keep an eye out for their bright, checkered wings!

HOW THEY FLY: Frigga Fritillaries fly close to the ground to escape cold northern winds.

CATERPILLAR: The Frigga Fritillary caterpillar is black with dark spines. It has a purple line running down each side of its body. It likes to nibble on willow leaves and mountain avens.

DURING THE WINTER: Frigga Fritillary caterpillars hibernate during the winter as partly grown caterpillars and continue their life cycle the following summer.

FLUTTERING FACT: The name "fritillary" comes from the Latin word *fritillus*, meaning a chessboard or dice-box. It is thought to refer to the checkered markings on the fritillary's wings, which help the butterfly soak up the sun's warmth on the cool tundra.

# Dingy Fritillary
## *Boloria improba*

 Wingspan: 28 to 34 mm

Upper Side

Underside

The Dingy Fritillary looks like a smaller, dirtier version of the Frigga Fritillary—like a fritillary that's taken a roll in the dust! In fact, its scientific name, *Boloria improba*, means "inferior fritillary," referring to its dingy appearance! The Dingy Fritillary appears quite brown when it flies. Closer up, its wings are a muted orange-brown with faint, dark markings. On the underside, its wings are light brown with a wide grey band on the outer part of the hindwings. The tops of the hindwings are marked with white.

WHERE TO LOOK: The Dingy Fritillary is found on the tundra from Alaska to southern Baffin Island, Nunavut, and as far north as Melville Island in the Northwest Territories. It prefers low, wet places where sedges and dwarf willows grow.

HOW THEY FLY: Dingy Fritillaries fly slowly and stay close to the ground.

CATERPILLAR: Dingy Fritillary caterpillars have not yet been described in North America. In other places, they are described as being dappled brown with reddish-brown bristles and a cream-coloured line on the upper side of the body. Butterflies lay their eggs on the stems of dwarf willows. The caterpillars eat the leaves when they hatch.

DURING THE WINTER: This butterfly takes two years to develop from an egg into a butterfly. Caterpillars hibernate twice. The first time is during their first winter, when they are young. They hibernate a second time as mature caterpillars. They become butterflies in their third summer.

FLUTTERING FACT: Lepidopterists (people who study moths and butterflies) call the Dingy Fritillary a "true tundra butterfly." In the springtime, it is one of the first butterflies to appear on the tundra. During the cool Arctic summer, its dark colours help it soak up the sun's warmth.

# Ross's Alpine

*Erebia rossii*

 Wingspan: 31 to 34 mm

Upper Side

Underside

The Ross's Alpine is a very dark, blackish-brown butterfly. Near the tip of each forewing, there are two dark spots with white centres. These spots may be outlined with orange or red and can look like the number "8." The female may also have another row of small spots on both wings. On the underside, the hindwings are dark brown with a jagged grey band near the outer edges.

WHERE TO LOOK: The Ross's Alpine is found on the tundra from Alaska to northern Labrador and as far north as the southern Arctic islands. This northern butterfly prefers wet, boggy, and shrubby places on the tundra where sedges grow.

HOW THEY FLY: The Ross's Alpine flies low over the ground with a slow, bouncy flight.

CATERPILLAR: The caterpillars of many alpine species have not been described. The ones that have are dull-coloured and are lightly striped or plain. They have large heads, and their bodies taper into two short "tails." This caterpillar likes to eat sedges, including scorched alpine sedge and looseflower alpine sedge.

DURING THE WINTER: Many northern species of alpines take multiple summers to become butterflies. Partly grown caterpillars hibernate for the winter and continue their life cycle the following summer.

FLUTTERING FACT: The Nunavut communities of Taloyoak, Baker Lake, Clyde River, and Iqaluit each have a very similar general name in Inuktitut for butterflies and moths: *saqakilitaaq, haqalikitaaq, tarralikisaaq,* and *tarralikitaaq.*

# BANDED ALPINE
*EREBIA FASCIATA*

 Wingspan: 38 to 53 mm

Upper Side

Underside

The Banded Alpine is a dark, medium-sized butterfly. Its wings are dark brown with a blush of red in the centre of the forewings. On the underside, the wings are brown with bold, light-coloured bands.

WHERE TO LOOK: Banded Alpines are found on the Arctic tundra from Alaska to the coast of Hudson Bay and as far north as Victoria Island and Banks Island. Look for them in wet places where cotton grass grows.

HOW THEY FLY: Banded Alpines have a slow, fluttering flight. They fly only short distances when disturbed.

CATERPILLAR: These caterpillars are green with black patches. They have dark brown heads and are covered in short hairs. Alpine caterpillars feed on grasses and sedges. While the caterpillar food plants are not known for this species, Banded Alpine butterflies are often found near cotton grass.

DURING THE WINTER: Many northern alpine species take multiple years to become butterflies. Young caterpillars hibernate during their first winter. They hibernate again as mature caterpillars during their second winter.

FLUTTERING FACT: Among some Inuit in Nunavut, rubbing a butterfly or caterpillar on a baby girl was believed to help her sew beautiful designs when she grew up.

# Polixenes Arctic

*Oeneis polixenes*

 Wingspan: 33 to 51 mm

Upper Side

Underside

The Polixenes Arctic is a medium-sized butterfly that varies in colour across the Arctic. Its wings can be yellow-grey to orange-brown and are slightly see-through. There are usually no marks on the upper side of the wings. However, sometimes the wings can have a row of small orange spots or one or two dark spots. On the underside, the hindwings are a marbled grey-brown with a darker band through the middle.

WHERE TO LOOK: The Polixenes Arctic is found on the tundra from Alaska to Labrador and as far north as the southern Arctic islands. This northern butterfly likes dry, rocky, and grassy areas and tends to gather in groups, or "colonies." You will have to look closely to spot this butterfly. The camouflage colours and patterns on the underside of its wings help it vanish into the tundra as it basks with its wings closed.

HOW THEY FLY: The Polixenes Arctic flies for short distances, stopping to land on small rocks. When frightened, arctics lift quickly into the air and let themselves be carried away on the wind.

CATERPILLAR: These caterpillars have greenish-yellow heads with six dark stripes. Their bodies are striped in grey, black, and tan, with a greyish-green stripe running down the back. Female butterflies lay their eggs on grasses and sedges. Caterpillars have been known to eat both kinds of plants.

DURING THE WINTER: Young caterpillars hibernate during their first winter. They hibernate again as mature caterpillars for a second winter before they become butterflies. Arctic caterpillars can dry out all of their body tissues and freeze solid, thawing in the spring when the Arctic warms again.

FLUTTERING FACT: True to their name, arctics are among the toughest of butterflies when it comes to surviving the cold. Beyond the North American Arctic, they can be found in many high, cold places from Europe to Mongolia, Siberia, Russia, and the Rocky Mountains.

# COMPTON TORTOISESHELL
*NYMPHALIS VAUALBUM*

Wingspan: 52 to 70 mm

Upper Side

Underside

The Compton Tortoiseshell is a large, beautiful butterfly. It has jagged, golden-brown wings that are darker in colour at the base. Bold, black marks pattern the forewings. The hindwings have a large, black spot that is partly bordered in white. On the underside, the wings are a marbled brown and grey with a silvery white "V" in the centre of each hindwing. The camouflage patterns on the underside of the wings, along with the jagged wing shape, help this butterfly to disappear among dead leaves or bark.

WHERE TO LOOK: Compton Tortoiseshells are mainly found in woodlands across the northern United States and south of the tundra in Canada. However, these brave butterflies have been spotted from mainland Nunavut to Alaska and are known to wander into the tundra as far north as Baker Lake, Nunavut! Keep an eye out for this butterfly in Arctic towns, and you might see it poking around buildings, looking for a place to hibernate at the end of the summer. Tortoiseshells also sometimes gather around puddles and wet patches of ground. While they drink from flowers and willow catkins, you might also see them feeding on rotting fruit, sap, or even animal droppings.

HOW THEY FLY: Compton Tortoiseshells are fast, dashing fliers. They have been described as being very difficult to catch!

CATERPILLAR: Caterpillars are light green and speckled. Black spines on their bodies help them defend themselves against predators. They feed together in groups on willow and dwarf birch.

DURING THE WINTER: Tortoiseshells store up fat in their bodies for the winter. They find sheltered spots like the eaves of buildings or cracks in rocks to hibernate. When they emerge in the spring, their wings are torn and tattered. Only after they have hibernated do they find a mate and lay their eggs. Because tortoiseshells hibernate over the winter as adult butterflies, they are likely the longest-lived butterfly in Canada.

FLUTTERING FACT: Some kinds of butterflies, including tortoiseshells, raise their body temperature by shivering. On chilly days, a few minutes of rapidly shivering their closed wings can heat up their flight muscles enough for them to fly short distances!

## Tips for Identifying Arctic Butterflies

Most butterflies of the Arctic tundra belong to one of the following groups: the sulphurs, the coppers, the blues, and the brush-footed butterflies. The brush-footed butterflies are a large family that includes the fritillaries, arctics, alpines, and tortoiseshells. To help you place an unfamiliar butterfly into the proper group, some questions to ask yourself are: Is the butterfly small, medium, or large? What shape and colour are its wings? How does it fly?

### Sulphurs
• Mostly medium-sized butterflies
• Yellow, orange, or green wings with simple wing patterns
• Often have a small silver spot in the centre of the hindwing
• Fast, fluttering flight

Coppers and blues are "gossamer-winged" butterflies—named for their delicate, shimmering wings. The males are usually brightly coloured while females are more dull-coloured.

### Coppers
• Small-sized butterflies
• Shiny, reddish-brown or orange wings with black markings
• Strong fliers

### Blues
• Small-sized butterflies
• Rounded wings
• Males usually have bluish wings; females are darker
• Underside patterned with dark spots and bands
• Often have a weak, fluttering flight

The brush-footed butterflies are named for their front pair of legs, which look like tiny, fuzzy brushes.

## Fritillaries
•Mostly medium-sized
•Orange, dark-checkered wings with beautiful patterns on the underside
•Fly close to the ground

## Arctics
•Medium-sized
•Dark grey or brownish wings with camouflage patterns on the underside
•Pointed forewings and rounded hindwings
•Short antennae and hairy bodies
•Bob up and down unpredictably as they fly

## Alpines
•Small- and medium-sized
•Dark brown to black wings, usually with lighter patches of red, orange, or brown
•Broad, rounded wings
•Fly low with a weak, fluttering flight

FURTHER READING:

*Butterflies of the World* by Adrian Hoskins

*Common Insects of Nunavut* by Carolyn Mallory*

*Kaufman Field Guide to Butterflies of North America* by Jim P. Brock and Kenn Kaufman

*The Butterflies of Canada* by Ross A. Layberry, Peter W. Hall and J. Donald LaFontaine

*The Butterflies of the Northwest Territories* by the Government of the Northwest Territories

*Source for Fluttering Facts on pages 28 and 30

ACKNOWLEDGEMENTS

Special thanks to Ross Layberry for permission to use some of the natural history details found in *The Butterflies of Canada* and for providing helpful comments on the draft manuscript. Many years of patient work by dedicated lepidopterists have provided what we know about northern butterflies today. For inspiring wonder, I am grateful for the butterfly exhibits at the Natural History Museum in London, England, for the Monarch Butterfly Biosphere Reserve in Michoacán, Mexico, and for the butterflies that graced my own Arctic trails in the most unexpected moments.

AUTHOR

Mia Pelletier studied ecology and anthropology and holds an MSc from the Durrell Institute of Conservation and Ecology in the United Kingdom. Drawn to wilderness and shorelines, Mia has lived in faraway places from California to the Magdalen Islands and the Canadian Arctic and spent six years working on the co-management of Arctic protected areas with Inuit communities on Baffin Island. *A Children's Guide to Arctic Butterflies* is her third Arctic natural history book for children.

ILLUSTRATOR

Danny Christopher has travelled throughout the Canadian Arctic as an instructor for Nunavut Arctic College. He is the illustrator of *The Legend of the Fog*, *A Children's Guide to Arctic Birds*, and *Animals Illustrated: Polar Bear*, and author of *Putuguq and Kublu*. His work on *The Legend of the Fog* was nominated for the Amelia Frances Howard-Gibbon Illustrator's Award. He lives in Toronto with his wife, four children, and a little bulldog.

INHABIT MEDIA
IQALUIT · TORONTO

A CHILDREN'S GUIDE TO
ARCTIC BUTTERFLIES